PATTERNS IN THE DARK

by

Mary Sheeps

CW00341511

Mary Shee

Typeset and published by
The National Poetry Foundation
27 Mill Rd
Fareham
Hants PO16 0TH
Tel: 0329 822218

(Reg Charity No 283032)

Printed by
Meon Valley Printers
Tel: 0489 895460

Cover illustration by Graham Rust

Sponsored by Rosemary Arthur

For: C.E.W.S.
and our children --
unfailing source of love,
laughter, and support.

'Time to Straighten Your Tie' first appeared in
'Acquainted With the Night' (A year on frontiers
of Death) by Allegra Taylor, Fontana/Collins.

'Awareness' was set to music and performed by
Caroline McCausland.

'Interior Decoration' won Ist Prize, Humerous
Poem, in the Wharfedale Music Festival 1989

Poems in this book have also appeared in:
Farmer's Weekly, The Field, Pennine Platform,
The Anthology of New Christian Poetry, Orbis,
The Countryman, Envoi Summer Anthology 1990,
Aireings, and Pause.

ISBN 1 870556 01 1

£4.00

CONTENTS

Morning is on red alert.
News of invaders has reached
The oystercatchers, who streak past
In formation, sirens screaming
And flash white lights against the blue.
A woodpecker revs up its drill
In trees where builders
Unaware of restrictive practices
Hammer a new day into shape.
Our chauvinistic cockerel calls the hour
And summons the faithful to lay.

Balsa poplars swing censers
Down the aisles and breathe
Pink smoke through the larches.
The river tunes its strings
As the sun climbs on the rostrum;
Wood-pigeons stroke the air
With velvet voices but mallard
Surge full throttle up the wind.
My dogs rush to keep appointments
With unwilling clients
And decode urgent messages.

I am an autumnal onlooker
Among this April activity,
But green memories stir of days
When delight blazed in the sky
And cast long expectations
Over uncut grass.

Sitting on the step small round and fair
Chattily choosing his words with care
He asked her: "Did you know?
There's only one God. Did you know?"
She answered speeding to the end of the row:
"Well dear, everyone's got to share."

Knit one, purl one, knit two together;
Shadrach, Meshach, and To-Bed-You-Go.
Sitting on the step, old age and youth
She may have hit on a very great truth.

I think I will send her to
The Ayatollahs for Christmas.
"Not much use dears carrying banners
If you won't make way for Mr Manners."

Perhaps I may send her to
The Reverend Paisley and the Pope.
"Give and take dears." What a hope!

I shall send her to Thatcher and Gorbachov.
"Put those toys away and don't show off."

Knit one, purl one, knit two together;
Shadrach, Meshach, and To-Bed-You-Go.
Sitting on the same step, age and youth
She could make them all cardigans
Of homespun truth.

BUTTON UP YOUR OVERCOAT.

My neighbours regard poetry
With suspicion: it smacks
Alarmingly of undressed souls.
They feel much safer if souls
Are buttoned into winter overcoats.
A hint of spiritual décolletage
And they scuttle off
Embarrassed as crabs.

Why muffle emotion under
Cautious hats and layers
Of thermal knickers?
Wearing a poem might make
Their hearts fly on the bubble
Of a willow-warbler's call
Or grieve on the sorrowing wings
Of an owl's adagio flap.

If they kicked their shoes off
And ran barefoot though verse
They might dance to blues
Rendered by moody trees,
Catch water-lilies at prayer
On pools of mystery;
Glimpse the reflection
Of each other's hearts.

But then of course, they might
Quite possibly, just catch a chill.

Five grey men
Meet by the river-side.
Cold winds of espionage
Blow round about them;
They hunch their shoulders
Against knives.

Expressionless
They exchange secrets
Through thin beaks and are
Impersonal as station waiting-rooms.
They reek subversively of menace
And the dark.

Cautiously the secret police
Approach with binoculars,
But the men were always
Watching out for them
And disperse quickly
But with no apparent haste.

Loosely attached
As cigarette ash and
Rising casual as smoke
They take to the air,
Their drab anonymous raincoats
Flapping out like
Monstrous wings.

They nearly fooled me,
Those spies:
I could have sworn
They were herons.

My grandmother taught me
To play Russian roulette
While she lay in bed
Smelling of luxury and violets.

Her weapon was an ivory box
Lined with russet wood
Carved and fragrant
Dangerous as a pistol;
Under its inlaid lid
Texts stood to attention
Small cartridge scrolls of hope and fear
Close ranked and packed with dynamite.

"Choose only one," she'd say
Reclining in quilted silk,
Breakfast tray on knees
Not giving second chances.

"If I can pick the verse
With angels' wings
I may fly safely through the day
But here are also words that kill.
Will they explode inside my head
And blow me up?"

It was well understood
Her time was precious:
"Hurry up darling make a choice."
The voice was ripe with yawns.
Small fingers trembled on the trigger.

My pulse still starts to race
When I smell sandalwood.

RARE BIRDS
A Rondeau

Too rare a sight to see him fly
Blue shriek, green gasp and fiery cry
And watch him plunge his skewer wit
To spear fun on the end of it
While shoals of laughter minnow by;
Then shaking carefree arrows dry
Arrest the current with his eye.
Too rare a sight!

Children with nets of hope may try
To scoop out star-fish from the sky
When fires of fantasy are lit,
But as years pile on bit by bit
Daydreams and kingfishers grow shy:
Too rare a sight.

BORROWED TIME

We live on a very expensive loan
Sometimes I wonder whether
We can keep the payment up:
The question swings a pendulum between us.
We hear its slow insistent tick
But do not talk of it.

Once we swigged laughter together,
A bubbly intoxicating brew
That has become too strong for you;
Now we share quiet amusement
A soft still drink
But not without danger.

We no longer dance
But the room is wreathed in Verdi.
Eyelids pulled by a single string
Spring to release a glance
That flies between us
On a special note;
Simultaneously individual axes
Fell a stubborn cross-word clue
And I forget our mortgage rate.

ACCIDENTAL DESIGN?

Frost ferns ice window panes
Grown-ups in mellow mood
Allow a messy ploy:
Too cold to venture out again.

Fingers pleat pristine paper
Thumb-pressed precise
Then splash a random radiance
Of paint across the crease.

Long minute's agony of waiting
While it dries! Open to
Ghosts with trailing fingers
Strange flowers, monsters' wreaths.

Abstract artists of the nursery
New avenues perceived
Scream with delight:
"Oh look at mine!"

How did God feel
After releasing a rampage of greens
To fold a page of snow
And see revealed

His new design
Cushioned miraculously
On this white expanse:
Wild cyclamen leaves?

AWARENESS

I hear the sound of thistledown floating
Listen and hear the spiders spin.
Tune your ears to green grass growing
With the silver sound of a violin.

Feel through your fingers the snowflakes' whisper
Breeze on your cheek from a butterfly's wing
Touch the petals of falling roses
Dance to music that song-birds sing.

Marvel at pearls in rain-drenched flowers
Diamond dews and feathers of frost
Watch on the wind for sea-birds sailing
Search in the fire for dreams you have lost.

Miss Havisham walked through
The wood last night.
Wisps of her trailing veil
Are snagged on brambles
Her tattered wedding dress
Has caught on trees
And paranoia drips
From sodden branches.

Miss Havisham reeks
Of terrible revenge:
Her scary breath is
Stronger than street-lights
And can obscure the sun.
She creeps on unsuspecting
Travellers to cram
Her cruel cobwebs
Down their throats.

I dread her muffled laugh
Of poisoned spite
Her soft-shoe shuffle tread.
She lies in wait
And hangs about in hollows.

I hope she will not
Linger in my head?

Sixteen horses, conker-shiny fit
And autumn ripe, strings tuned
For equine melody on stubbled stretch;
An elderberry sheen on hunting boots
Of men not wearing sporting pink
But urban yellow tabards over blue.

Hounds, strangely wolfish, have a handler each.
A helicopter hovering overhead
Is falconer's hawk with swivel eye to scan
And talons keen for prey.
They hunt a man.

I try to weigh two terrors in my mind:
That of the girl spears sirens through my eye
I smell her panic pain, can not forget
Defiling brutishness which turned to sewage
That which should be stars.

Now he is coursed like fox or hare
But unlike theirs his crime
Is not existence. It is rape.
And yet, and yet ... watching this net
Close round our woods and fields
A particle of me wants
His escape.

Birch branches shake in silvered green
And grass has turned white-haired with dew
Rose-window cobwebs filter dawn;
From poplar trees neurotic tall
'Blue-grey' a wild wood-pigeon calls.
A blind grey mist that floats and sways
Strange ectoplasm hides the lake
Then fumbling softly gropes away:
Grey mystery at break of day.

But shadows menace evening light
When stars arrive to frost the night.
Cold graves beside the churchyard wall
Stand sombre sentries; grey with pain
The watching faces of the sick
Wait to be charged with hope again.
Industrial plaque bodes aching teeth
For sooted stonework bleak as bones
And rain of grey self-pity falls
If laughter truants out of call.

Grey balances the dark and light
A watching waiting clouded breath
That hangs between the great extremes;
Waiting for birth, awaiting death.

KINGFISHERS

Lazing beneath a silver olive tree
I've often been alerted by
The urgent whistle of your horn-pipe cry
And stretched my eyes to watch you fly
Perfectly camouflaged between
Ionian sea and azure feathered sky.

You are not colour-matched to Yorkshire skies.
Over the slaty Wharfe you go
A prism shot from charged high-voltage bow
To race the river's breakneck flow:
Then you are jewelled in between
Cold grey above and mirrored grey below.

A floral chintz with a delicate air
I think, don't you, for my bedroom chair
But dare I have the carpet mauve
Like Lady Fresco's house at Hove?
Old bitch, though I could never stand her
I covet her trompe l'oeil verandah!
Now shall I have a Roman blind
Or pleated curtains, interlined?

The bathroom's next; that must be done.
Bathrooms can give one endless fun
There's even quite a lot of scope
In matching loo-paper with soap.
And darling! How's this for an idée:
A goldfish swimming in my bidet?
I wonder if gold cherub taps
Would be a little much perhaps?

I always think it such a pity
To make a drawing-room look too pretty.
Sophistication is the rage
And nothing looks as smart as beige:
I hope I've hit on just the thing
In seven different shades of string.
I flogged our Meissen to buy lots
Of chic Victorian chamber pots.

Do come and see our gilded Aga
Obtaining that was quite a saga!
I died when Algie found the bill.
I haven't used our charcoal grill
Since our au pair, the silly nut,
Burnt the cork tiles and then she shut
The budgie in the microwave:
Selina's being awfully brave.

Yes darling, husbands are so funny
They simply hate one spending money
And Algie's views are really quaint:
He says he doesn't like new paint!
That damp patch on his study ceiling
Gives him a cosy lived-in feeling.
He leaves his wellies in the hall
The poor lamb has no taste at all.

This boring hall could take a mural
Something simple but wildly rural
With birds and bees and an urn or two.
I'm always mad about urns, aren't you?
When I've done the house from hall to attic
Life is sure to be dreadfully static.
I hate to feel I'm in a groove.
I must tell Algie ... we'll have to move!

In these rooms
Objectives have no limit
But progress is celebrated
In centimetres.

Most of the telephones
Are scrambled and rag-doll limbs
Require support,
But cheerfulness keeps rising
On thermal currents of laughter.
Shadows are not allowed
To loiter here, where optimism
Is a five-hundred watt bulb
And despondency gets vacuumed up
Each time it tries to settle.

Yet sometimes I need callipers
To hold my spirits up.

Great choirs of snowdrops
Mass to prayer
With chaste Gregorian
Treble chant.
One daffodil kicks up
Its skirts
In wild erotic
Pagan dance.

The snowdrops
Look at it
Askance!

To all the air I vainly cried:
"This octopus possession strangles me.
Can't I be loved and love
And still be free?"
But no one heard or listened
None replied
Until upon the green horizon of my view
You came to stand.
The bird of all my loving flew to you.
You held it for a moment
In your hand,
Then opening up your fingers
To the sky you said:
"Our love is liberty.
Feel free to fly
But know that I am true."
Because you never tried
To pinion it
The bird of all my loving
Stays with you.

Draped in expensive silk of feather grey
The valley wears September like a shawl;
A scarf of birdsong flaunts about its neck
Jet beads of blackberries glitter round its throat
But oh my Love of many summer days
How frayed and wintry now your wind-thin coat!

The ever fashion-conscious countryside
Which always keeps its wardrobe up to date
Knows it will sport a bright new dress each May,
But time's run out for me to hope and cling
Or try to patch again the wearied cloth
That will not last you for another spring.

Can I be strong enough to wave goodbye
Dressed in the laugh you've always loved so much
And try to keep my tears for underclothes?
I wish that I could unstitch all the pain
That you have worn so long with such panache
And make your sad rags whole and new again.

Those who read my lines
Risk laminitis.
You said I rhymed too much
Which made the verse as lush
As fields of clover,
And what is more
(I must not say moreover)
Verbosity spells literary disaster.
The rhyme should be the servant
Not the master.
I will give up arpeggios
And stick to chords.
Poetry should travel light
Be airborne spare restrained:
Nouvelle Cuisine
With no whipped cream.
But I get drunk on words!
I will take a vow
Of verbal abstinance:
Go on a diet, and only
Write poetry
In Lent.

(For Laurence Cotterell)

AT NEEDLEPOINT

You hold your life
Together with stitches;
Force frayed thread
Through the narrowing eye
Of each day's sharp needle
And ward off death
With a bodkin.

Once you climbed mountains
Hit boundaries served aces;
Planted avenues of poplars
Nurtured Loderi St.George
And grew exotic fruit.
You pruned trees from the top
Of a tall ladder.

Now with great effort
You dig embroidered gardens
And labour in herbaceous
Needlepoint. Each vanquished row
Is the end of a tournament
And you ski down your precipice
On a strand of wool.

They are very beautiful
These new flowers you grow;
You still use green fingers
But cultivate strange plants
In an unlikely climate
And nothing can unravel
The tapestry of our love.

(For C.E.W.S. - 8.4.89)

Be careful with prayers:
They can be dangerous, ignite unexpectedly;
Perhaps they should carry
A Government Health Warning.

Hearing of your friend's death
As he dropped a dry fly
Over a rising trout
I said:
"Oh Pa wouldn't you like
To go like that? To cease mid-stream
Mid-cast, no long farewell?"
You were horrified. Not for you
Such wild untidy impulse of departure.
"That is not how I want to die,"
You said.
"Before I meet my Maker
I would like time to straighten my tie."

And it was granted you!
Oh it was granted you
This wish, this dangerous prayer:
Two long painful years, while the flesh
Was honed to the bones
But your tie was straight
So very straight.

You showed me much:
The values of integrity, humility,
Unfailing courtesy ... the brash
Could bark their shins on your politeness ...
And you were master of the soft answer
That may turn wrath away but can annoy.
Old fashioned virtues, yours,
But not the worse for that.
If you were too fastidious for compassion
Which is essentially an earthy gift
Then you were still exceptionally kind.
You had a flair for laughter:

22

Your wit a kingfisher's beak
Humour a syncopated rhythm.
You showed me words:
Always in set metre, patterned rhyme
But words that had a ring.
You did not teach me how to have a fling.

Was it a comfort to you, your faithful,
Disciplined, pew-steady Churchianity?
I really do not know; support possibly yes
But comfort, sadly no. If consciousness
Survives the jumble sale disposal in the earth
I hope you got a wonderful surprise.

I hope some infinitely gentle angel greeted you
(Surely not God who must be hierarchies on).
I hope it said:
"My dear chap! Lovely to see you!
You must be quite exhausted. Come on in."
I hope it said:
"Your laces look so straight
Do slacken them, it's quite informal.
Judgement Day? There's no such thing.
It's D.I.Y. You've judged yourself too hard
These last two years. Besides we're modern here:
Continuous Assessment, not exams.
Sin? Why yes, perhaps you ought
To learn to sin a little bit,
You who were always so afraid of it.
There are a few harmless ones that you may care
To re-evaluate sometime. But later
Not just yet; you are too tired
And we're so very pleased to see you."

Was it like this? I'd like to think it so
But oh alas! One thing that's certain is
I do not know.

(G.W.N. for D.W.N.)

23

His was the saddest funeral:
There was no grief.
One or two attended, sparse teeth
In the church's gaping mouth
But there were no mourners.

He occupied his house
For a full span but
Only a snail's trail
Marked the years.
No light shone from his windows
And he took care
That none should enter;
Always a north-facing man
He slammed his door
For the last time in May.

Next winter a congregation
Squeezed into the same pews
And bled all down the aisle
For the plucking of a dayflower
Who pushed her small green shoot
Into many hearts and left a hole.
Her brave candle flickered
For seven years then
Guttered out on Christmas Eve
But the echo of its light
Illuminates a village.

(For Diana and Tim)

BRIMHAM ROCKS

Great dinosaurs you stand
As positive as malice and as dark.
Some age when phoenix hatched
And dragons flew, when ice-age maidens
Held their crystal breath,
Wombed in Earth's belly
Prisoned sunlight grew
Until its rage ripped wide the crust
That tried to cage it. Chaos ran
Fire-blood beneath the sun
And your volcanic vastness
Was begun.

Impudent trees have danced
Upon your face, only to fall
Because the wind's wild sickle
Would not cease. Clouds drift
And seasons pass; old houses crumble
Grass and bracken die, yet you remain
Constant as death and old as birth
And weird as all the mystery
Of these two.

Now children scramble up
Your monstrous sides
To set the air alight
With bird-song laughter.
Perhaps by day their picnic jollities
Castrate your old malignant potency,
But I have stood among your lumbering shadows,
Breath stopped, hair rigid, heart pneumatic drill
And heard your ghostly grunting to the moon.

UNEXPECTED EXCHANGE

Imperious battering on my window pane
Wakes me at dawn.
But who can reach that height
In my tall house?
Not Don Giovanni, that's for sure:
He knows my age.

Draw curtain: fierce Saracen
Has stormed the castle wall
And strides the sill, attacks with sword
For battle to the death, fancied crusader.
He does not know he strikes at his own image
Which I replace with mine,
Glad that stout sheet of glass
Protects my eye from fish-hook bill.

His chestnut back is burnished saddlery
Breast feathers master's metalwork,
Lap tight as fish scales
Painted precisely as the Book of Kells.
Eyeball to eyeball
Each mesmerised, we gaze.

I step into his tiger lens
To know a different world:
No sticky sentiment
But rapier sharp perceptions.
I lean upon the air
To choose my menu in the grass below.
I hover, dive and kill
Accelerate the sky.

Before he turned to fly
Did he read poetry
Through my mild eye?

SNAILS

Watching that snail
Slime slowly up a rock
You must not mock
Its cautious and lugubrious pace:
Perhaps beneath the staid protection
Of a mottled shell
There beats a heart of fire!
Perhaps fierce pulses race
And bright imagination sings
That it could soar and dare
Perform such feats
Achieve such things
That it might be
A super snail ...
A snail with wings!

So if it cannot cast aside
Its little safeness,
Shed its mobile house
And climb sublime to Himalayan height
Do not deride
Its effort. For who knows?
To me it seems
Quite possible
That even snails
Have dreams.

THE SHIP OF THE MOUNTAIN
Llong-Ar-Y-Mynydd

My childhood navigated mountain waves
Through bedroom window,
Flew over fields and farms to swarm
Twigged rigging netted on winter sky
Hoisted leaf sails billowed by summer gale
To steer a legend's galleon over Wales.

Once centuries before
An ash-key fitted in Snowdonia's lock
Had launched a frigate on round Pen-y-Gaer.
(Grown-up, we found it marked on ancient map.)
Did earlier children pace its decks like us
Stow unicorns and dragons in the hold
And carry cargo of their dream-spun gold?

As soon as eight year legs grew stout to trudge
Long gap of miles stretched between house and hill
Brave expectations of impending voyage went wild;
Some moons are safer cried for than embarked on:
Triumphant, tired, we reached our magic sea
But Llong-Ar-Y-Mynydd changed back into tree.

(For my mother, with love)

A flame disc balances on morning's rim
I hold my breath in case it slips:
It looks precarious.

Mist on the river is oriental silk
Trees compose themselves above it
To drink green tea and discuss abstracts;
They bow to each other with infinite courtesy.

Air at sunrise is made of rice paper
Goldfinches sketch pagodas with fine pens
Strike temple gongs under curled eaves
With bright precision.

Scent from wisteria waves a fragile fan.
The sky in my garden is thinnest porcelain
Ringing with peonies and spikes of blossom;
If I touch it will it break?

Laburnums hang gentle laughter on the breeze
But my weeping pear cries silver tears
Of great restraint; it never gives way
And sighs softly at my weakness.

I must be careful not to fall inside the frame:
I might trip and spoil the tranquility.
I wish I was inscrutable, my heartache
Hidden in a wide embroidered sleeve.

Bright serpents twirl
About the sky
And hiss forked tongues
Of effervescent stars:
Children are waving sparklers.

It is a scary game
Played against the night
But full illumination
Waits their call.
They touch a light switch
And normality returns.

James cannot reach that switch.
His stars fizz out and fluctuate
Not being strong enough
To steer by: he struggles down
The tunnel of his mind
Trips up on loose connections
Tries again; we watch
With pride and pain
As he makes a private pattern
Whirling his sparkler
In the dark.

(For Belinda and Charles, with love and admiration)

I will plant a butterfly garden:
No ordered rows, these petals fly
Light-hearted in unbordered skies
Flutter herbaceously in space, wings bright
As stream of holly-hocks in flight, to stay
A hover-cloud of all my dreams
For just one day.

I will grow Tortoiseshells:
Sweet-scented cottage flowers
Mottled with orange, hot as sun-drenched brick
On which a net of summer shadows falls;
Bold Cabbage Whites to roister pollen wine
From licensed buddleias open on a wall,
And Common Blues who mirror
Sky above and grey shell sand below
Shall be the laughing barefoot ways I love.

Yellow Brimstones next: a clump of sparks,
To jump-start darker days
And glancing Swallowtails of streamlined grace
As swift and fragile as a carefree hour;
Perhaps a Painted Lady's flirty face
Preening among my aerial grass
Might use each dew-filled blade
As looking-glass.
I will need hot-house space for travellers' tales:
Try Purple Emperors stamped with golden rings
And sow flamboyant Peacocks, strangely marked
With mysteries of the Orient on their wings.

I will plant butterflies, but not to last.
Commitments honk impatient horns outside
But in my garden it's so quiet that you may hear
The silent song of one escapist day
See colours that a rainbow cannot catch;
And you shall stay and share the magic I have made
Till thieving dusk steals light and shadows creep
And all my day-dreams fold their wings
In sleep.

COMMAS
Polygonia C-Album

Fuse-wire legs are angled fine
As geometrical design;
Wings tattered as a vagrant's cuff
Are torn and dusty, hedgerow rough;
Small punctuation marks in white
Slivers of moon, the only light
On wings which fastened up can hide
The harvest bonfire that's inside.

In winter months they hibernate
In undeciphered coded state
Among the tickets dropped by trees,
And well disguised as one of these
They fool grub-hungry birds whose eyes
Rake autumn litter for supplies
Till summer's well-oiled key unlocks
The secrets in their tinder-box.

Half a pound of fear and hate
In half a pound of treacle
Makes religious activists:
Pop go the people.

Rock the cradle rule the world;
Baby Bunting's learning
Greed and power are petrol bombs
To keep the home fires burning.

Round and round the mulberry bush
Politicians crawling;
Jack and Jill went up the hill
But acid rain was falling.

Here we go gathering nuts in May
No thought of conservation
So long as it's not in my back yard
Who cares about starvation?

If you go down to the woods today
You may not find a tree.
Teddy bears can't picnic there:
Nothing left to eat you see.

Four and twenty embryos
All planted in a row
Are fertilized with toxic waste:
Funny, they don't seem to grow.

Girls and boys come out to play!
Watch your parents fighting.
Your turn may come another day
Isn't that exciting?

"Religion dear?" she asked
Consent form held
Below her sterile smile.
"Christian," I answered:
One can always hope.
"It means WHAT DENOMINATION, DEAR,"
She said.
"Christian," I tried again
Lying in silly bath-cap, baby's gown
Awaiting my Pre-Med.
She thought me simple in the head:
"No, no; that isn't what it means.
What Church do you attend?
I need it for my file."
"CHRISTIAN," I bellowed
Cross, unchristian-like.
"I worship God in any church
It's all the same to Him
If not to us."
She said I must not make a fuss:
They had to know which minister
To call in case I died.
Such words of comfort!
"Let them all come to save my soul
I'll need their prayers if I am dead.
Religion isn't rationed yet," I said.
"They'd want to know about the burial,"
She answered, sharper now,
Thinking me frivolous.
"We meet all sorts!":
Eyes roll towards her friend.
A needle brought our conversation
To an end: I had no time to pray.
"Just put her down as C. of E."
I heard the sister say.

This is the morning for looking at lace:
I have waited impatiently for fifty-one weeks
And at last the cupboard is unlocked.

First green lace! Oh to wear green again!
Just to see it, once a year, draped on silver poles
Is to breathe consolation through my eye.

Pink lace is delightful: a champagne flirtation
Pirouettes and raspberry sorbet; all frivolity
And not to be despised for that,

But white lace freezes my breath with beauty:
A cold hush of star petals whispers of brides
And shrouds and frightens me with strangeness,

Asks who will come to try on Christening robes
Or stretch thin hands to finger winding-sheets
Before next Lace Week turns another key
To throw its fine-thread questions over trees.

We took the pack and cut the cards
And drew the Queen of Spades:
Dark portent; doom.
Then hissing cobwebs menaced us
From corners of the room;
The skeletons of bats took wing
And rattled through the air
To pour their shadows in our cup.
Beware! Take care!

We fanned the pack and cut again
And drew the King of Hearts:
Love's sovereign cure.
The gremlins from the moon's blind eye
No longer sounded sure.
The giddy stars turned cartwheels
And taught the flowers to jive
And syncopated sunbeams boogied:
"Laugh and give!"

If we could stack the pack and choose
What cards would we arrange?
No dark, all light?
But these are linked as surely
As morning is to night;
I'd risk the grief and keep the hand
We drew so long ago,
Our love and pain are intertwined,
So close they grow.

Then expectation hung upon each day
Like early dew
Trembling with greyhound eagerness
Upon the grass.

Then we could pace the wind
Or be as one with breathless summer days,
And we could hear the singing in the sky
And read the changing patterns
On the river's face.

Strong magic came in simple things:
Gnarled stones or moon-smooth pebbles
Feathers, leaves.
Then sticks were swords
And every tree a castle.

But oh with age the third eye
Starts to close.

Suffering is organic:
Dug into the trench
And well forked in
Unexpected flowers
Are often forced
Out of the compost heap
Of great distress.

But Evil, what of that?
Surely Evil is not biodegradable.
The perpetrators of it may be
We have to hope for that;
Given exposure to the light
They too may be re-cycled
Rotted down and changed
For ultimate forgiveness.
But Evil, the thing itself
That hangs round horror tips
An empty plastic bottle
And will not decompose?

Is it like polythene
Only to be consumed
By fire?

JANUARY

January is the month
For grudging hospitality:
It's such a grumpy old curmudgeon
Such an uninvited guest
Who doesn't know when to go.
January makes me yawn
And look at my watch
Allow lapses in conversation
While it maunders on relentlessly
Unmoved by my rudeness.
It brings out the worst in me
I want to stick a knife
Between its shoulders
And push it over the step.

But sometimes, very occasionally
It comes armed with a perfect present
Gift wrapped in blue and white:
A day of dry white wine
So frosted from the freezer
That its cork is pushed out.

Oh, then I forgive it!

We dragged words
To the writing class,
Varnished against criticism
But porous inside for praise.

She brought a little box
Of blue stained-glass.
"Just help yourselves,"
She said, "Please pass
It round." It went
Politely held, from hand to hand
With some embarrassment
For at first sight
It looked quite empty:
Nothing there to take.
Then we began to understand
That it was filled to overflowing,
Crammed with light.

She gave us, free,
Translucent trinket
Stocks of knowing,
Shared them from her long
Viewing point
At ninety three.

(For Genevieve Oliver)